TO THE TEACHER

The THEORY DRILL GAMES are designed to teach Musical Rudiments in an **interesting and attractive manner, while saving valuable time during the lesson period. All the** work is done at home, and the teacher can quickly evaluate the pupils' efforts as the work sheets are handed in for examination.

It has long been recognized that the quickest and best way to master NOTATION, TIME, RHYTHM and all other elements of music, is by means of WRITING EXER- CISES. Unfortunately, the theoretical side of music study is usually the least attractive, from the student's viewpoint, and the difficulty has been that of capturing the interest and attention of young pupils to the point where they are willing to do the work by them- selves at home.

To help overcome this difficulty, the work has been presented here in the form of MUSICAL GAMES or PUZZLES. It offers a DO-IT-YOURSELF plan in that each step is described pictorially in the form of ANIMATED DRAWINGS or COMIC STRIPS, so popular with the average child. This obviates the necessity for lengthy explanations during the lesson period and, at the same time, injects a bit of humor into what otherwise might be considered a "dry" subject.

The Games are presented in LOOSE-LEAF form, and it is most important that the pupil be given ONE LEAF AT A TIME, not the whole book at once. In this way, the drawings and musical puzzles contained in future games will retain their newness and come as a surprise to the pupil, who then looks forward with anticipation to each successive lesson. For identification, the pupil's name should be written on the front of the folder in the space provided. The set of papers is then kept in the studio and assigned *one game at a time* at the desired intervals.

It will be seen, at a glance, that the THEORY DRILL GAMES are equally adaptable to private or class instruction.

John Thompson

CONTENTS OF BOOK ONE

THEORY DRILL GAME, No.
The Keyboard

Pupil's Name_____   Grade (or Star)_____

W.M.Co. 7358   Date_____

2

4.

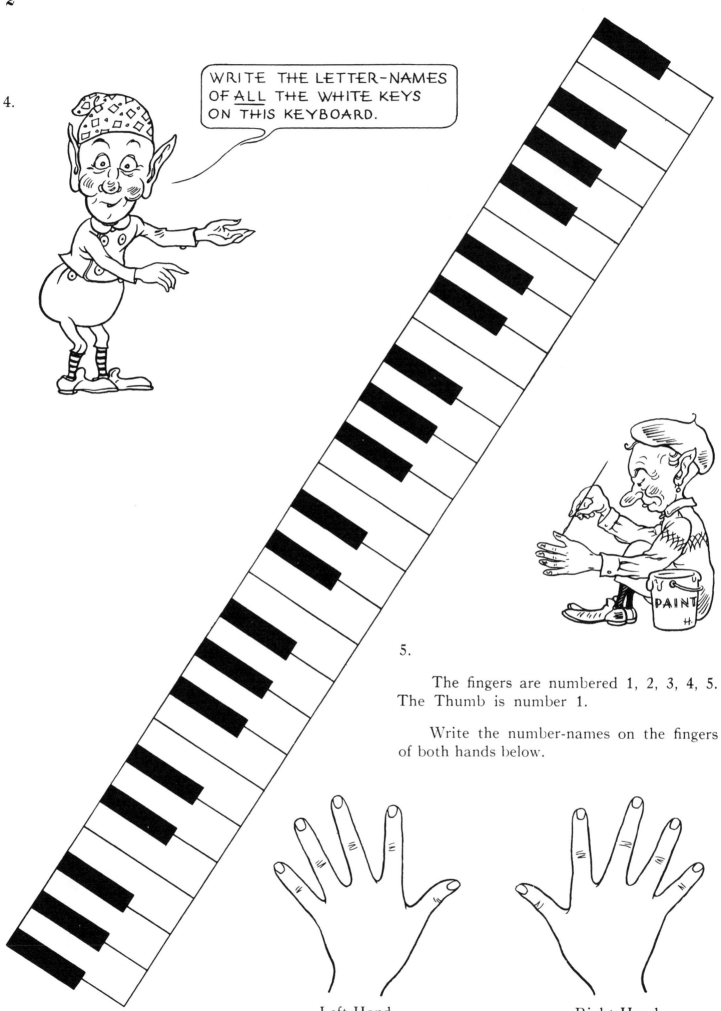

WRITE THE LETTER-NAMES OF **ALL** THE WHITE KEYS ON THIS KEYBOARD.

5.

The fingers are numbered 1, 2, 3, 4, 5. The Thumb is number 1.

Write the number-names on the fingers of both hands below.

Left Hand   Right Hand

THEORY DRILL GAME, No. 2

The Clef Signs

Pupil's Name⸺⸺⸺⸺⸺⸺⸺⸺⸺ Grade (or Star)⸺⸺⸺⸺

The Treble Clef Sign

1. Trace over the dotted lines in the exact order shown above.

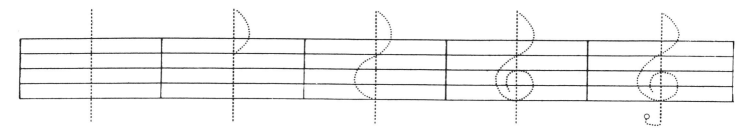

2. Trace the first three Clef Signs, then try it without the aid of the dotted lines.

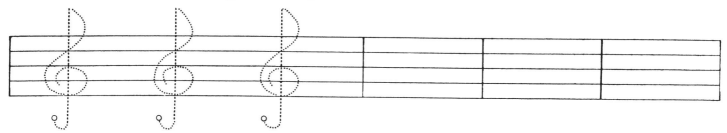

W. M. Co. 7858   Date⸺⸺⸺⸺

The Bass Clef Sign

3. Trace over the dotted lines as shown by the little gnome above.

4. Trace the first three Clef Signs, then draw three "on your own".

5. Draw the following:

Treble Clef	Bass Clef	Treble Clef	Bass Clef	Treble Clef	Bass Clef

THEORY DRILL GAME, No. 3

Time Values

Pupil's Name_____   Grade (or Star)_____

1. Write beneath each note the number of COUNTS (or Beats) it gets.

   <u>4</u>   __   __   __   __   __   __   __   __   __   __

2.

Write a four-count note here.	A one-count note here.	A two-count note here.	A three-count note here.

3.

Write a Quarter Note here.	A Half Note here.	A dotted Half Note here.	A Whole Note here.

Date_____

Line Notes

Space Notes

THEORY DRILL GAME, No. 4

The Grand Staff

Pupil's Name_____   Grade (or Star)_____

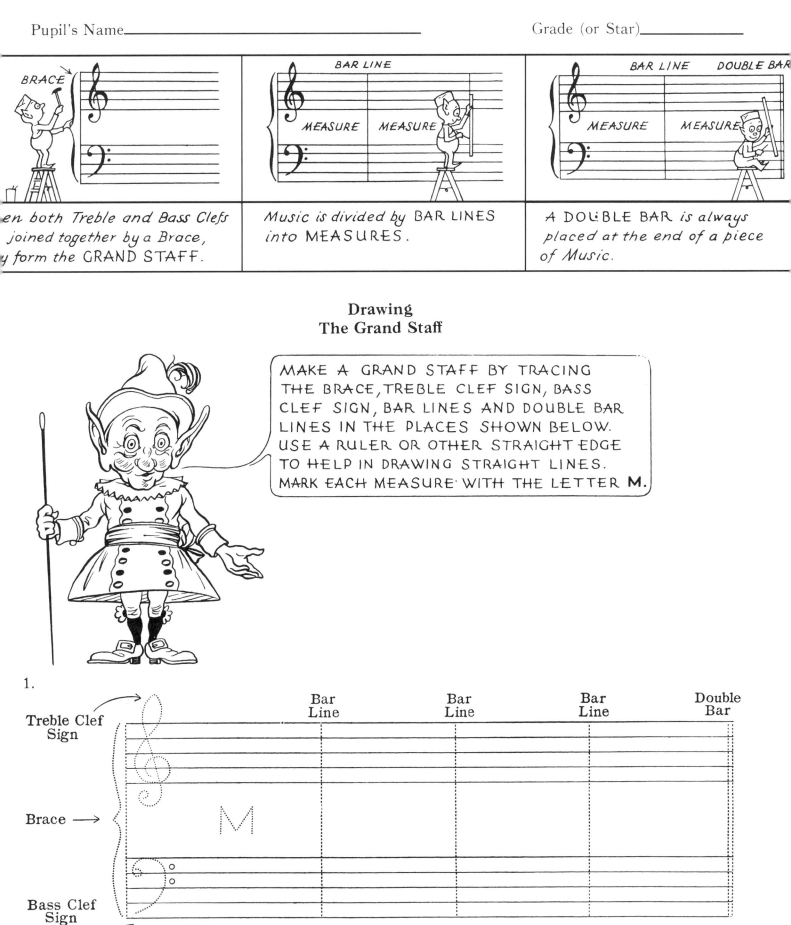

en both Treble and Bass Clefs joined together by a Brace, y form the GRAND STAFF.

Music is divided by BAR LINES into MEASURES.

A DOUBLE BAR is always placed at the end of a piece of Music.

Drawing
The Grand Staff

MAKE A GRAND STAFF BY TRACING THE BRACE, TREBLE CLEF SIGN, BASS CLEF SIGN, BAR LINES AND DOUBLE BAR LINES IN THE PLACES SHOWN BELOW. USE A RULER OR OTHER STRAIGHT EDGE TO HELP IN DRAWING STRAIGHT LINES. MARK EACH MEASURE WITH THE LETTER **M.**

1.

Treble Clef Sign   Bar Line   Bar Line   Bar Line   Double Bar

Brace →

Bass Clef Sign

W.M.Co. 7358   Date_____

Time Signatures

2. Trace the Clef Signs, Time Signatures, Double Bars and Braces below.

 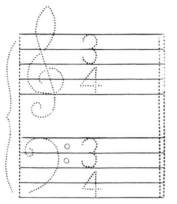 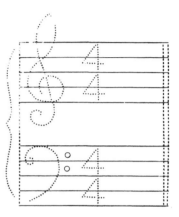

How many counts?_____   How many counts?_____   How many counts?_____

3. Write the counts for each measure in the following examples.

4.

THEORY DRILL GAME, No. 5
Note Writing

Pupil's Name_____   Grade (or Star)_____

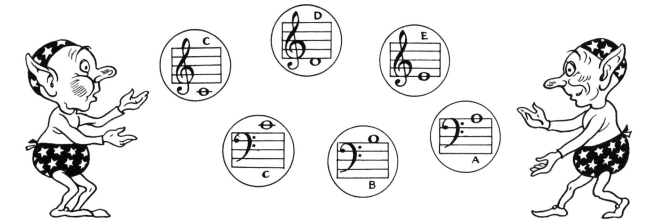

1. Trace the notes in the first measure, then copy them and write their letter-names in the next three measures.

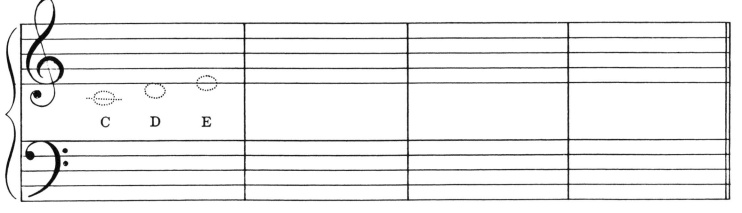

C   D   E

C   B   A

2. Write the letter-names of these notes.

Letter-names:

W.M.Co. 7358   Date_____

THEORY DRILL GAME, No. 6
New Notes

Pupil's Name_____   Grade (or Star)_____

1. Trace the new notes in the first measure, then copy them and write their letter-names in the next three measures.

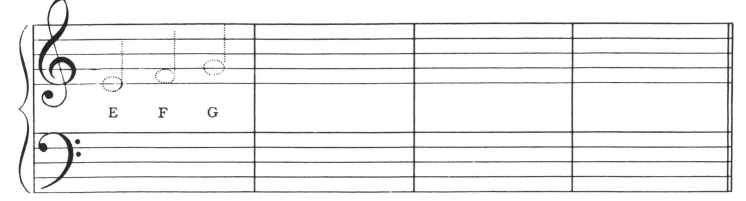

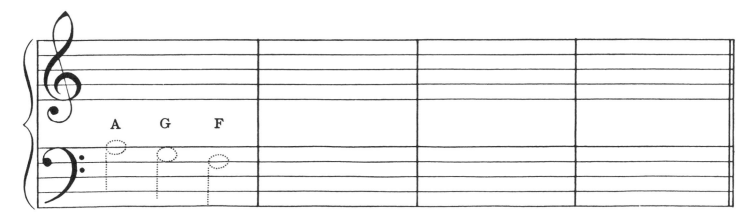

2. Write the letter-names of these notes.

W. M. Co. 7358   Date_____

3. Write the counts for each measure in the following.

Count:

4.

Count:

5.

Count:

YOU KNOW WHERE F AND G ARE IN BOTH TREBLE AND BASS.
SEE IF YOU CAN WRITE THEM (IN WHOLE NOTES) IN BOTH CLEFS.

6.

Write F in both Clefs. | Write G in both Clefs.

W. M. Co. 7358

THEORY DRILL GAME, No. 7

Pupil's Name——————————————— Grade (or Star)——————

1.

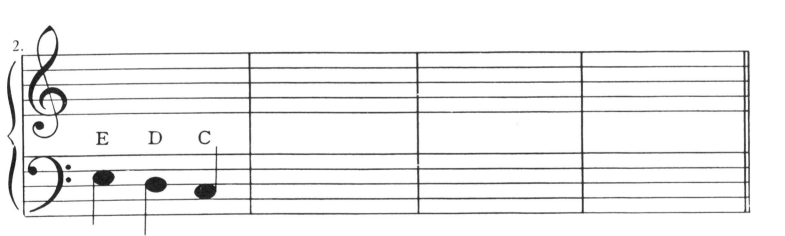

2.

3. Write the letter-names of these notes.

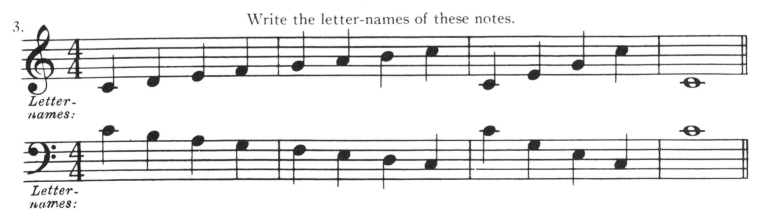

Letter-names:

Letter-names:

W.M.Co. 7358

Date——————————

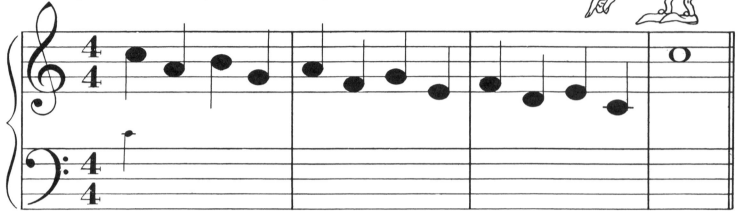

WRITE THESE NOTES ONE OCTAVE LOWER (OR HIGHER) AS DIRECTED BELOW. THIS IS CALLED TRANSPOSING.

4. Transpose to Bass Clef (one octave lower).

5. Transpose to Treble Clef (one octave higher).

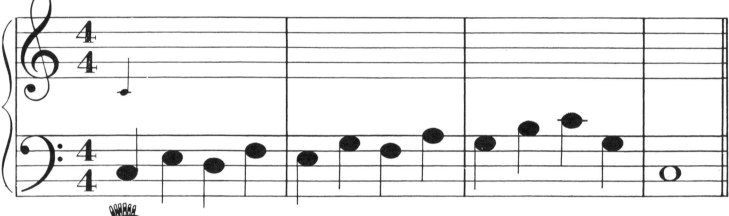

WRITE EACH OF THESE NOTES IN TWO PLACES, ONE IN TREBLE AND ONE IN BASS CLEF.

6.

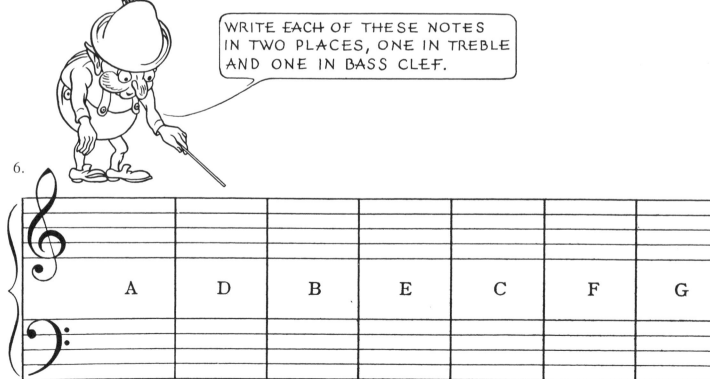

| A | D | B | E | C | F | G |

W. M. Co. 7358

THEORY DRILL GAME, No. 8

Pupil's Name _____   Grade (or Star) _____

The Garden

1.   Some words in this story are spelled musically. Write the letter-names below the notes.

While helping their [notes] in the garden, [notes] and [notes]
(letter-names)   – – –   – – –

asked for a [notes] of seeds to plant their very own little [notes] of flowers
            – – –   – – –

along the [notes] of the vegetable patch. Soon the pretty flowers grew, and one day they
          – – –

saw a [notes] gathering honey to store away and [notes] upon during the winter
      – – –   – – – –

months. They watered the flower [notes] each day and [notes] special
                                – – –   – – – –

flower [notes] to the soil.   With the coming of Fall the flowers [notes]
       – – – –   – – – –

and to their great dismay, they were all [notes] when the frost arrived.   But
                                          – – –

[notes] told [notes] and [notes] they could plant another garden in
– – –   – – – –   – – –

the Spring.   Copyright, MCMLVI, by the Willis Music Co.
                            International Copyright Secured
W.M.Co. 7358   Printed in U. S. A.   Date _____

Write the counts to these measures.

2.

Count:

3.

Count:

4.

Count:

Puzzle Pix

Can you write (in whole notes) the names of the objects shown in the pictures—in both Clefs?

5.

THEORY DRILL GAME, No. 9

Pupil's Name_____   Grade (or Star)_____

1. Draw the Bar Lines

Date_____

4. Write these notes in both Clefs (in whole notes).

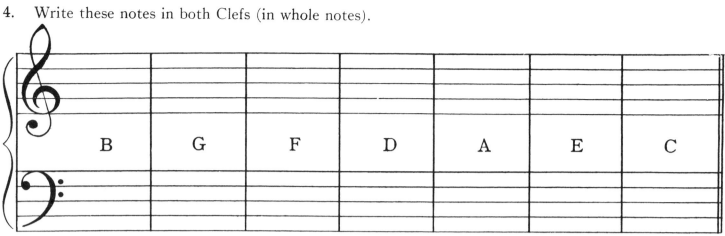

| B | G | F | D | A | E | C |

5. Write these notes in both Clefs as directed.

Whole note.	Two Half notes.	Four Quarter notes.	Dotted Half note.
E	G	F	A

Puzzle Pix

6. Spell (in half notes) the objects pictured in the puzzle—in both Clefs.

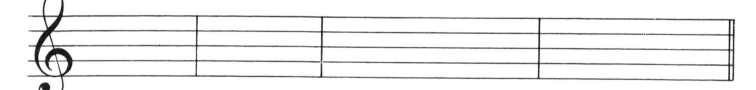

THEORY DRILL GAME, No. 10

Rests

Pupil's Name——————————————————   Grade (or Star)——————————

Whole Rest   Half Rest   Quarter Rest

A whole measure's rest.   Gets 2 counts.   Gets 1 count.

The Whole Rest hangs from the 4th line like a monkey on a tree.   The Half Rest lies on the 3rd line like a pussy cat.   The Quarter Rest looks like a Sea Gull in flight.

1. Trace.   Draw four Whole Rests.

2. Trace.   Draw four Half Rests.

3. Trace.   Draw four Quarter Rests.

W.M.Co. 7358

Date——————————

HOW MANY COUNTS TO EACH REST?

Write
- W FOR WHOLE REST
- 2 FOR HALF REST
- 1 FOR QUARTER REST

4

1   W

W   2

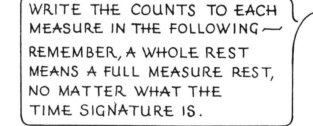

WRITE THE COUNTS TO EACH
MEASURE IN THE FOLLOWING —
REMEMBER, A WHOLE REST
MEANS A FULL MEASURE REST,
NO MATTER WHAT THE
TIME SIGNATURE IS.

5.

Count:

Count:

Count:

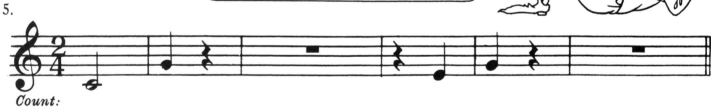

THEORY DRILL GAME, No. 11

Pupil's Name_____ Grade (or Star)_____

> DRAW BAR LINES IN THE PROPER
> PLACES IN THE FOLLOWING EXAMPLES –
> DON'T FORGET, A WHOLE REST MEANS
> A WHOLE MEASURE'S REST.
> IT CAN BE A 2-COUNT MEASURE,
> A 3-COUNT MEASURE OR A
> 4-COUNT MEASURE.

1. Draw in the Bar Lines.

2. Transpose these notes to the Bass.

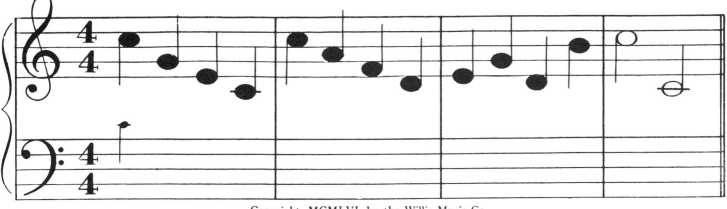

W.M.Co. 7358

Date_____

from
"Lullaby" by Brahms

3. Transpose to Treble.

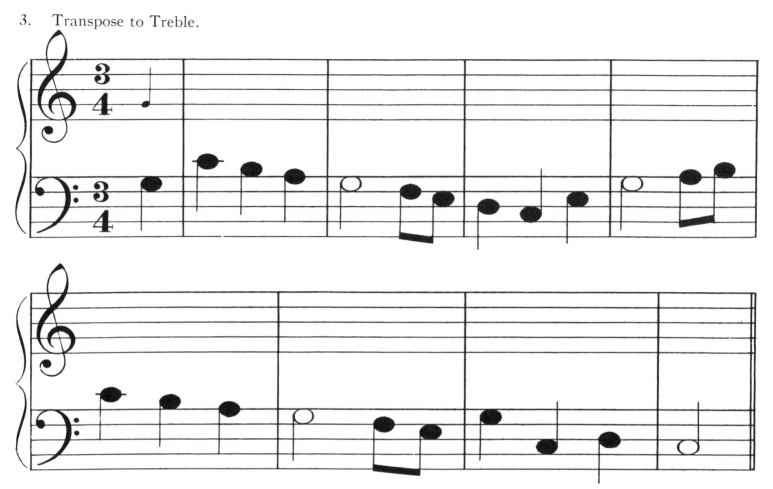

Puzzle Pix

4. Find a word in each picture that can be spelled in notes, then write it (in whole notes) in each Clef.

THEORY DRILL GAME, No. 12
Accidentals

Pupil's Name_____   Grade (or Star)_____

1. Trace the Signs and Notes in the following and notice particularly how the Signs are placed *exactly the same as notes* when they are on the lines or in the spaces.

2. Write the letter-names of the following.

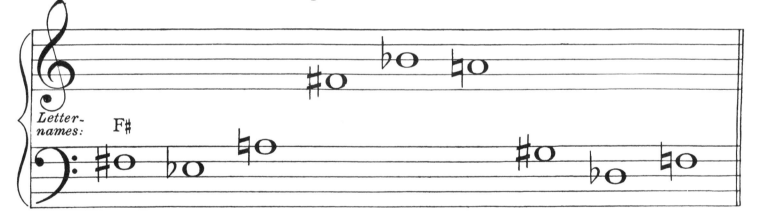

3. Write these notes in both Treble and Bass.   (Whole Notes)

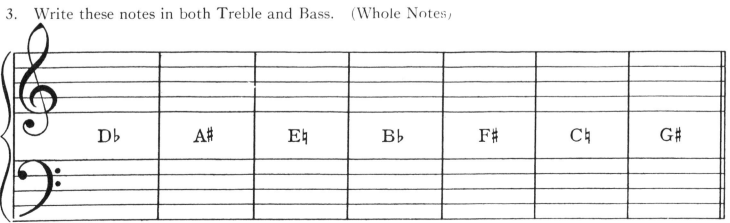

W.M.Co. 7358

Date_____

A Day at the Circus

4. Complete the story by writing the letter-names of the notes on the lines below.

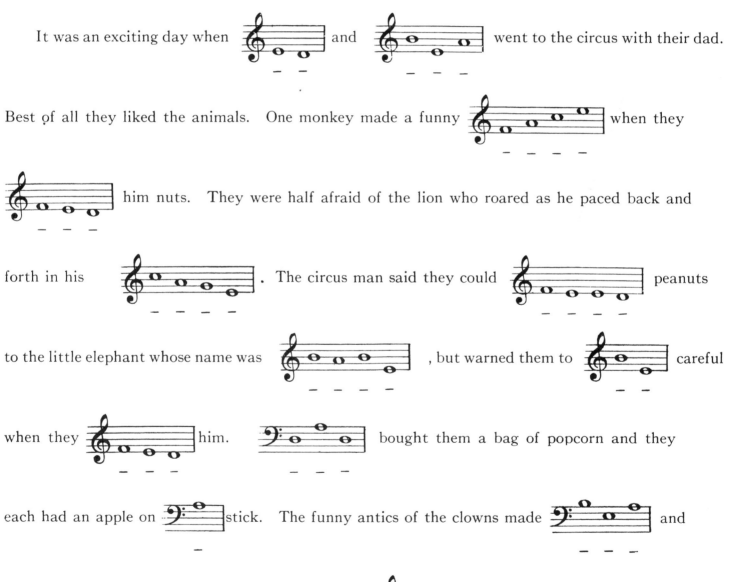

It was an exciting day when ⟨notes⟩ and ⟨notes⟩ went to the circus with their dad.

Best of all they liked the animals. One monkey made a funny ⟨notes⟩ when they

⟨notes⟩ him nuts. They were half afraid of the lion who roared as he paced back and

forth in his ⟨notes⟩ . The circus man said they could ⟨notes⟩ peanuts

to the little elephant whose name was ⟨notes⟩ , but warned them to ⟨notes⟩ careful

when they ⟨notes⟩ him. ⟨notes⟩ bought them a bag of popcorn and they

each had an apple on ⟨notes⟩ stick. The funny antics of the clowns made ⟨notes⟩ and

⟨notes⟩ laugh. To make the day complete, ⟨notes⟩ bought them each a balloon to

take home.

THEORY DRILL GAME, No. 13

The Eighth Note

Pupil's Name_____   Grade (or Star)_____

1. Change each of these Quarter notes into Eighth notes by adding a hook on the right side of the stem.

Make Eighth notes in pairs by joining the stems.

2. Write notes having different counts as directed below.

A 4-count note.	A 3-count note.	A 2-count note.	A 1-count note.	A ½-count note.

3. Write the counts in the example below.

Date_____

THE EIGHTH REST LOOKS LIKE THIS 𝄾 IT IS EASY TO REMEMBER BECAUSE IT IS MADE LIKE THE FIGURE 7.

Trace	Draw

4.   Draw the Rest Sign for each of these notes.

Rests:

5.   Write the counts.

Count:

Count:

Another Spelling Bee

6.   Write these words (in whole notes) in both Clefs.

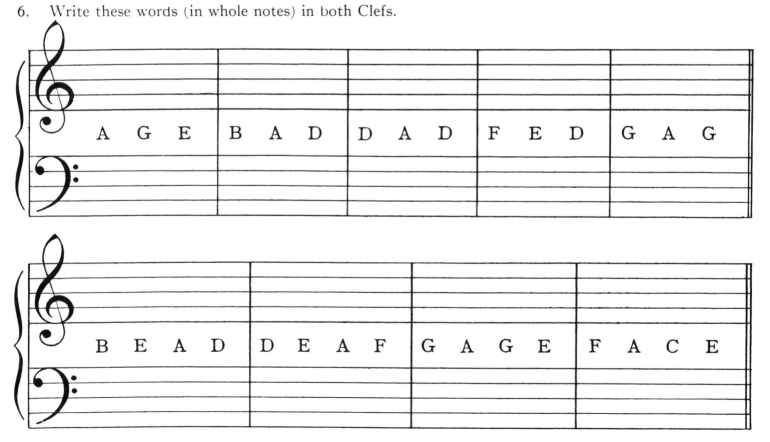

| A G E | B A D | D A D | F E D | G A G |

| B E A D | D E A F | G A G E | F A C E |

THEORY DRILL GAME, No. 14

Pupil's Name_____   Grade (or Star)_____

The Scout Hike

1.   Spell the musical words as before.   Be careful of the Accidentals as they form part of the story.

It was [music] November day when Uncle [music], the Scout Master,

took Troop [music] for a hike.   He found [music] stone and taught them how to rub a

knife blade on it to make [music] [music] Uncle [music]

showed them how to make a [music] of coals to cook the [music] th / had

brought along.   While they were eating, a little dog came and [music] for some

[music] so they [music] him.   This was [music] thing for

them to do as they were always kind to animals, and Uncle [music] said that was their good

[music] for the day.   As the sun went down, they started home with a smile on every

[music] and went to [music] well [music] and happy.

Date_____

W.M.Co. 7358   Copyright, MCMLVI, by the Willis Music Co.
International Copyright Secured
Printed in U. S. A.

There is one note missing from each measure in the following.

It will be either a ♩ or an ♪ note.

Write in the missing notes.

BE SURE TO EXAMINE THE COUNTS! THIS WILL HELP IN FINDING THE RIGHT NOTE.

2.

Counts: 1 2 1 2 1 2 1 2 1 2 1 2

3.

Counts: 1 2 3 1 2 3 1 2 3 1 2 3 1 2 3 1 2 3

4.

Counts: 1 2 3 4 1 2 3 4 1 2 3 4 1 2 3 4 1 2 3 4

5. Spell these words in both Clefs, using the kind of note shown below the letters.

FEED BEEF EDGE ADAGE

THEORY DRILL GAME, No. 15

Writing Time Signatures

Pupil's Name_____ Grade (or Star)_____

1. First write the counts, then put in the proper Time Signatures.

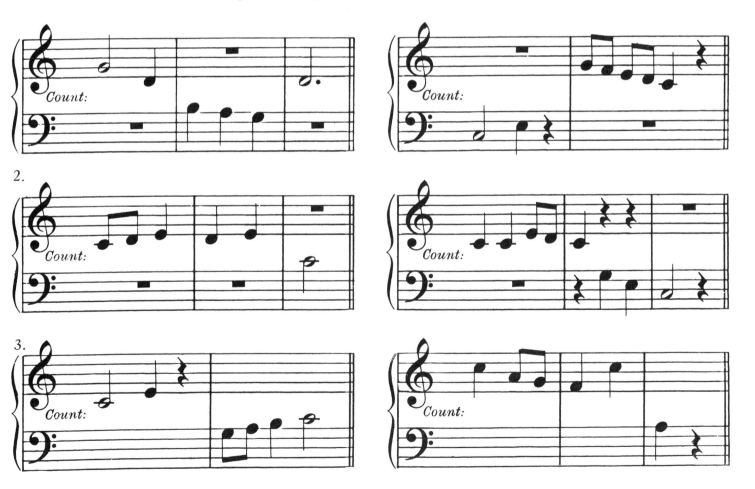

W.M.Co. 7358

Date_____

4.

Counts: 1 — 2   1   2   1   2   1   2   1 — 2   1   2

Counts: 1 2 3   1 2 3   1 2 3   1 2 3   1 2 3   1 2 3

Counts: 1 2 3 4   1 2 3 4   1 2 3 4   1 2 3 4   1 2 3 4

5. Write the name of the note to which the Accidental belongs.

G#

6. Put the proper Accidental before the note indicated.

G#   E♭   F♮   C#   G♮   A♭   B♭   D♮   G#   C#

"Having successfully completed this book, the pupil should be assigned Theory Drill Games, Book Two."

W. M. Co. 7358